The Morning After Relapse

The Morning After Relapse
Copyright © 2016 Christina Hopp

ISBN-10: 1523262907
ISBN-13: 978-1523262908

Cover Artist: Karen Da Costa.
Contact: rendacos@gmail.com

The Morning *after* Relapse

Christina Hopp

John 8:36 HCSB
"Therefore, if the Son sets you free, you really will be free."

2 Corinthians 5:17 HCSB
"Therefore, if anyone is in Christ, he is a new creation; old things have passed away, and look, new things have come."

Psalm 51:17 HCSB
"The sacrifice pleasing to God is a broken spirit. God, You will not despise a broken and humbled heart."

A special thanks to the darkness of the world, the Light beyond, and the nights I shook with hope for a new day.

CONTENTS

AUTHOR'S NOTE

We all have different stories, but everyone 'relapses' or gives into old habits in some way or another. *The Morning After Relapse* is a book on the wonders of God's grace and gentleness when we are at our most vulnerable moments.

Here is my story of being won over by an encounter with God.

You aren't alone wherever you are.

- C

Liberation Pt. 1

you said you wanted to know me.

so here's me. bruises, whipping hands, punching myself silly until my ugly pops off like styrofoam pieces.

here's me. the one who still drowns in old oceans, sins, muddy puddles, salty taste. i swallow them like a third dessert, stuffed but never enough to fill me up.

a 3am time bomb. whispered prayers in the bathroom stall. rubbed off paint. static.

damaged goods. ruined righteousness. the holy grail snapped at the neck. the one pastors condemn when they warn you of withered roses.

i repent. "i was born this way, i can't hold back". salvation relents.

waning, dimming, losing.

innocence pours out of my sides like a blood sacrifice. and the alter shakes from my rage.

FORGET ME NOT

i could swear on
the grave of my innocence
the knife is too deep.

no matter how thick
blood is
it is too sacred
to cleanse me.

after all my tongue
has tasted and
hands have dug in,
you'd think the angels
would stop singing
of my redemption.

but heaven keeps going.
they know how this ends
and it isn't with death.

so though i am blind
and the shadows hover,
the future is a little brighter
with such ethereal beings
not giving up on me yet
and celebrating my freedom
before i have faced it.

what's the point of   religious dance

     if i am afraid of every mistaken step?

oh relapse. what a bloody demon.

          maybe the throne room has

some extra positions

             for minimum wage

so i can twiddle my thumbs

         in a place i don't fit in.

but what's the point

      of breathing faith

when i'm planning my own death sentence?

         if i kiss once, i'll kiss again.

if i die once, i'll surely die again. but,

   if i live, i live.   i only have one shot.

and i need something to show for it

         other than a refugee badge

from all the wars i ran from.

Untitled I

I wake with the remnants of a weaning moon
from the night before. The sky was inky,
like my palms after I reached into my
being. I felt nothing but darkness, new
in the most regretful of ways. I explored
the heart of my soul and found that when
I taste the ground, I taste the sweat
of my skin.
I am lost for good, but it isn't so good.
I wake with last night's shakes.
The adventure wasn't as long of a ride
as I expected it to be, and it scared me
that my evil wasn't at all surprising.

Slay me, slay me
for I am suffering
and if it kills me
to slaughter my demons
then there will be
more room
for you Lord
to shade me with peace.

Broken Vessel // Sinking Ship

hold back the trumpet sounds.
i'm not feeling well
and music so heavenly
deserves a heart that is willing
to dance to the melody.

quiet your voice.
for just a moment
hush the noise.
your words are a gem and
shouldn't be ignored
but i'm not feeling well
and i can't focus now.

shade your rays.
that glory you can't contain.
we both know i am unworthy
of your shining life upon my pain.

dry spells pass.
but my skin is crumbling
dissipating into sand.
i'm too far from the ocean
and wasn't given a map.
i'm not sure where i'm going
but it's more comforting
to be alone when i'm lost.

i'm not feeling well.
i don't need a righteous hand
or a crown of peace.
just understanding
that you're too overwhelming
and i am too weak.

Draining Myself With Bible Verses

Sometimes I think the devil is in me
and I can't flush him out. Just
a psalm a day, keeps the sin away
but what if sin is the veins and tubes
that protect a body from dying, what
if chiseling me down ruins me from
the inside out? I don't want to go, but
this isn't a way to live.
A psalm a day,
(if the weather is nice or when my
blood runs down the window like
teardrops, when I squeeze my eyes
with no release or find rest, rest, finally
getting some damn sleep after
quieting my arteries)
maybe keeps the sin away, at bay, or
just invisible for my vulnerability.
I don't mind the deceit, as long as
the devil is fooled to believe I'm
the victor, the one who found a way to
survive without a bloodstream.

Untitled II

under the piles i created with no one else to blame. responsible for my own undoing. in the stomach of the beast and the beast is within me. no pill extracts, no drink erases, all the regret, the sting, the betrayal in my kiss.

my virgin lips, my coarse epiphany, my warm heart. it's burning me, with affection towards things i shouldn't love.

so contradicting to everything i live for. so catastrophic to my redemption.

my capabilities are smothering. i seek rest from the pressure, the evil, the chances to wreck my salvation.

hungry, hungry, hungry. for something unfulfilling. but my emptiness is calling out and refuses to be silenced.

i need a straight jacket for all this sin. i'm tearing, scratching, fighting my way past holy. to be beaten down may be my only hope of strengthening.

THE LION'S FOOTSTEPS

so this is what it's like to vanish.

cold shattering on the floor
like forgotten last words
like a funeral for all our wonder.

he has a magician's hand
and I disappear in thin air.
I dissipate with the falling stars
and the comets have maps to all
us wanderers.

I tell them, no one wants me anymore.
and as the little girl across
the street swoons over their skylights,

they tell me how alone they are.

so this is what it's like to vanish.

a boiling regret but I'm not
hungry for soup. a dimming
vanilla candle on the edge of
·the bathtub.

I bury my head below the water.
that doesn't swallow the noise
but it muffles his footsteps just enough
to empty me out.

the drain slurps me like milk and
I'm okay with that.

I saw God at the other end of the

        store and checked the clothes rack to

seem busy.

           I could use another 50 dollar

      sweatshirt in a color I never wear,

it was better than the verse logo t-shirts.

          Running into old friends

is like plowing into a pit, pulling out the

        dirt you'd like to keep buried.

Like staring at a clothes rack and

         pretending you can afford it.

  Like seeing an ex and the air being filled

       with those late night kisses and it kills

you to see them act like it never happened.

       Like I'm the ex and God is wishing

I'd turn my head, He knows I hate yellow anyways.

writing of holy things is not second nature anymore / i wonder where my soft ran off too / probably melted from the metal / from the bitter i can't shake off / from the stone i etched my name on

i wanted to write a letter / "dear God, sorry we lost touch" / but i wasn't writing with much heart. much soft. / it felt like a whole new tongue was placed in my mouth / like meeting someone you haven't seen in a while / things aren't like what they used to be / but we're both too kind to say so

and isn't that the pin drop irony / even in the quiet / when the words are unraveling at my feet / i can still hear a lion's roar at the top of the cliff / and "dear God, sorry we lost touch" / somewhere echoing on the edges / bouncing into black holes and depths i can't reach

i don't mind the unfamiliarity in the silence / when it's like this / when it's so welcoming / so embracing / so transfixed on keeping me safe

let's not drown in our sorrow.
or in the anxiety of tomorrow.
fade away the woes loud enough
to vibrate your knees. quiet yourself
from joy killers. lay yourself with the
praying mantis, so still
(like an illusion)
as you beg for peace during the blaze.

THE SILENCE AFTER FALLING

i write this from the bathroom floor, with sweat and regret and all the things you'd expect to drip at 2am

i write this in the sanctuary, as pastor jokes about coffee being nectar from the Lord

while i wonder which burns more - the fury in hell or His grace for all my treachery

i write this and i'm kneeling but i don't feel guilty enough to speak

i write this with a dry tongue

and a ripple on my back for each time i thought i had won

i write this in my bed where i have sinned and i have prayed, an alter of the world morphed to heavens pit

i write this with a Bible weighing tons on my lap

i write this and i bite my pen

and there is nothing left to say.

God Never Gets The Hint When My Door Is Locked

i like praying with the lights off. no one can listen as i spill out burdened secrets. i sit on the earth as a nonexistent creature, with nothing to regret or marks to hide and the entire world spins like it doesn't need me alive, but in this room, blindness is better than seeing guilt trace me as thick as the hair on my arms.
just me and my voice, i reach out to darkness and know nothing will touch me, i will not be burned today. i pray for myself and my prostituted heart, from loving the skin of humanity to begging for deliverance but never really finding freedom. i sit with my demons, my support system, and shout at them for all the times i leaned on the last straw.

i repent for all the times i plucked it from God's hand.

i like praying with the lights off so i can shed my weight and expose the fading pulses within me that need reviving. as i reveal my inner deaths, it's more tender to this aching vessel than the glory that kills my evil.
God knows how to talk to me here, He's had training in the business of scared hearts. maybe there is a bell in heaven that rings when a beloved soul needs Him but the shivers are too much to withstand any more than this. maybe He knows just how to deal with me.
i like praying with the lights off. there is a gracious peace in the silence. i cover the physical so i can see the spiritual, and it is there. there in the presence of my wicked flesh and His overwhelming name, that i have hope of being redeemed.

I'M SO TIRED OF WAR

and carnality says her final words
in the billow, watery depths of grace.

it is something between "i knew
better than this" and "i couldn't
help myself". i am both body and
spirit. one is saved, the other follows
along on a floppy leash.
and as the soldier uniform stains,
it complains about the weather.

it's the uninvited guest but everyone
knows it's name. smile, wave,
acknowledge them. you don't let
people into your home without being
noticed. but the sin is breaking our
good lamps and drinking all the juice
from the carton.

and i don't know what to say
at the end of this poem
like all the other poems about washing
away the dirt. i think i need some
new rags, i'm just rubbing last week's
words on me now.

she sinks low into the soapy waters,
and only God knows what she whispers.

They Know Something I Don't

There must be a lot of he said-she said

> hearsay going on. Rumors floating

past the universes from heaven

> to hell, whispers about an overcomer.

It's got to be pretty mighty

> for this affair to be so public.

He must be onto something and it's

coming just above the mountain peak.

> God must see some potential in me

even in my weaknesses.

> Why else would my demons be

trying so hard to keep me down,

> unless they're scared of my victory?

Haven

just because you are hurting quietly, doesn't mean you aren't suffering. and when you finally begin screaming, it doesn't mean you aren't strong. your breaking point will be a bloody refuge, not a clean slate.

but you will be saved, you will live, someday you will get past your pain. you'll realize a good life isn't one without sadness but one where you find healing in the midst of it.

*Dear future sanctuaries, prayer rooms, alters, and anywhere
else God decides to lavish me with salvation,*

*I don't trust myself, not with these dams about to break loose.
I'm too fleshy to be protected from my addictions, too soft to
be a martyr for sacrificial love. Too weak to fight the natural
so let come what may. It's all otherworldly, the way grace is
expelling. If I survive, it was not by my imperfect doing. I'm
no hero. I'm not to be praised for standing, when the only
thing I'm capable of is putting myself in a grave.*

*You know. I am so unworthy. Who am I to place my feet at
Your door? Yet the welcoming mat states: There Are No
Enemies Here and it's suffocating how my wretchedness is
embraced.*

*But I couldn't ask for a better way to die. So I pinch my
nostrils and sink low. Without you, I am cold and numb to
any sort of feeling. Take me, break me, exhilarate me until
even my lungs expand differently. I ache with love and pain
when You are breathing in me.*

- C

don't panic

the alarms may ring
reminding of defeat
and maybe you regret
not listening to the red
flags
but there is hope
for we were born
with clenched fists and
screaming throats, breathing
in the sin of life the
moment we began

God never expected
perfection and He knows
the heart He created
it's not as dark as the
impurity laced in your skin,
in fact, you're shining
and He adores it
when you come to Him
just as you are
in your mess

so don't panic
embrace it
for God is timeless
and He has already saved
you from all you are
fearing

the flesh is weak and the spirit is willing / but what about when your flesh is more motivated / it sees the glorious wrath of the underdog / and would choose their rotting bones over cleansing any day

and as your spirit calls like a bird at dawn / who says you have enough strength to keep from covering your ears / who says you're free from falling back into such an ingrained nature / to ignore / to push / to clench and claw and shatter

that's what they don't tell you when you decide to cut yourself off / from the world / and the sting of death / there's still a sting, you just get pinched a lot sooner and a lot more frequently / with so much coming against you

but, i tell you, the race is worth it / it's so worth it / because life now is just a taste / and you get to decide the flavor / it's just a sprinkle of eternity / the topping of the ice cream cone / you haven't even gotten passed the first lickings

Son of Man

Jesus humanized himself.
He is not just the joy
you read in those
crinkled, biblical pages.
He cried too, you know, and
locked Himself away for days.

He had sorrow and pain.
No shame, no hate,
but was a Man who felt more than
overwhelming peace and a happy
face. He was more. He was human.
And He grieved. And He knows
how it feels
to be judged and condemned
and hurting
and murdered.

He was a walking healer but
a roaring anger.
More complex than what we think.

Not just a heart out for
the lost sheep, but also the one
tempted when
His body was weak.

And that's comforting.
To know the Man we worship
was at a moment in time
hungry.

And if He was hungry
then so can I be.
And if He found bread
without the devil's hand
then so can I find it
just as He did.

i have to prep myself up to pray

about my illnesses,

like an addict with her needle or even

writer with a pen,

like an infant that's screaming and

we don't know why,

like a sex worker during

a smoke break,

like a priest before he lights

the candles.

we all breathe in. exhale

anomaly, exhale deficiency, exhale

all of the aches that put a body

in the grave.

there is hope in our hesitant pauses.

YOUR FIRST PRAYER IS LIKE YOUR FIRST SMOKE

it's never a one time thing.

i know it's an oxymoron
            but i need a gentle God tonight,
      like in the last breaths of a hangover
            or an addict who whispers "i wish i
wasn't like this".
      soft,   like a heart chipping away
            into the black holes of my palms.
(the solar system could wail as the world
            is sucked into my shaking hands.
      i'd vacuum the dirt from the whole earth
            if i could, but i have enough to scrub
on my own as it is
            and i need a tender touch to fix my
problems.)
            i shake my head and curse
      all the habits i can't quit,
            but i wouldn't regret this relapse.
only a kind splendor,
            only a fingerbrush at your hem,
only a cloud's voice above the lightning rods,
            could shield me from this ache now.

He scattered the realms

for your deliverance

and searched beneath the

rubble for your name,

like a smitten heart plucking

out the prettiest rose.

He really is such a lover.

So if you ever feel

you're too sensitive, too

tender, too gentle,

too overwhelming, too soft,

too much for others,

just think, you have a

touch of God in you.

He marked you with a

holy taste.

THE DEVIL'S BLACK EYE

my anxieties are tombstones
but didn't Jesus sweat blood
didn't he beg God to
not forsake his soul

i am not alone
i have a prophet in my bones
a messiah for my name

a resurrected man who knows
just how i feel

condemnation isn't my fate

and even as the dog barks
of my inclinations
and even as i sleep with
ghosts on the ceiling,

there are sparks above my
weakness, power in my
stumbling
and it isn't evil

it is mightily good
like salvation for the homeless
a river for the thirsty

and my throat is croaking
but i still praise

Faith Is Losing The Warmth In Your Mouth After Saying His Name

but you keep on singing it anyways. even when you know death

is near, death is near, and you do nothing to save your

crippling salvation as your blood pours on the church chairs,

next to the woman who sings like it's with her last breath and a

man who quietly makes a cross to his chest. you keep singing

anyways. even when you don't care, even when you hate the

words and yourself and God for leaving you here in the desert

behind your eyes getting pecked apart by birds. they nip at you,

your veins, your heart, your sad excuse of a life source. they fly.

and you fly. but ecstasy always ends in a crash landing.

but you keep on singing anyways. even when you lose your

kneecaps after falling too hard. it's going to be dark soon and

you're stuck with your limbs lost in the mud. "you need to

clean up your stains," they tell you instead of picking you up.

"there are better places to find who you are," instead of helping you find your body parts. "don't fulfill yourself in these ways," they say, but you're so empty you're not sure you want anything else to patch your holes.

but you keep on singing anyways. in the back of a minivan with haloed christians, in your bedroom where you lost your innocence, as you read the breathing word that makes you feel nothing. you keep singing, because that's what keeps you living. you keep singing, hoping God is listening. you keep singing, because that's your calling. not to fit perfectly, not to scrub yourself away, not to find all your torn ligaments and hush the noise in your mind. just keep saying a name that is above your own even when it's the last thing you want to do. stare in the face of your relapsing world and sing to the only one that will rescue you.

Untitled III

in the dam of the day's anxiety. digging into vaseline bottles for more sticky fingers. cutting everything in arm's reach with my sharp edges and i need to be loosened, smoothness, renewal from my scratchy inclinations. i must swallow the churning, quaking, tremor.

release. throwing out half written drafts stuffed in my old back pack, with it's worn out edges, those god-awful edges. sucking on candy wrappers at my bedside for the excess sugar until my tongue turns blue. splattering paint on my skin to avoid doing anything else to myself that i'll regret.

air filter humming. bathtub draining. clean towel, clean face, clean socks that match my tongue.

this is my euphoria. finally cleansed.

what a sad bunch we make.
with sins we soon forget and
demons as our closest friends.
so fat with pride and lust,
how have we found room to
hate ourselves as well?
we lose our hope so easily
as though God is but a flame
that we ignite when we're ready
to prove our goodness, like He
doesn't know our nature, how
imperfect we are.

and what a loving Father He is.
to look at His very own, wrecked
by their own doing, with delighted
love, wishing we knew just how
willing He is to clean us up.

There was something in the air that day.
Like God was shaking the o-zone layer
anticipating the moment my eyes would be opened.
And when they finally were, it was a sudden shock.
My bones went from being a treasure trove for my sins,
to a vessel for the One who makes every tomb empty
by sacrificing Himself instead.

I couldn't contain the mighty pound in
my chest, like God was punching me
back to life, making me feel something again.
It was too much and yet not enough.
I scratched at my ribs and ripped myself open,
begging Him to resuscitate
every heart beat that was stopping.

They say it looked like a crime scene
when I bled to my hearts content,
but I see it as a final release.
A deliverance in the messiest of ways,
redemption from my old rusty blades.
An epilogue of glory, from death to saved.
So many angels sang that day, you'd think
they all gained wings.

But it was me, I gained angel wings.
Knee deep in the shreds of my old life fading,
I found sight of a love that never wanes,
never fails, never loses its step.
This love never forgets my name.
And in a ravaging storm and peaceful way,
it promised on this day
to save me always.

silence isn't a symptom
of being forsaken

in the quiet
you hear the angel call
soft, gentle
like a beating heart
reminding you there is life
in idleness and wait
there is good here
in the stillness

Glory showed it's face to death,
and with a lightning flash
a genocide of sin.

He laid where I should have been
on the wood where grace was shed.

The realm of hell flees at His name,
yet I, oh I, am to stand in His shade.

Wasn't He the martyr for my fate?
His last breath forgiving my
forsaken, straying soul.

Wasn't it I who closed my ears
when I was called to sing?
Didn't I kiss the feet of
all my fading whims?

The lust, the blood, the shouts of hate
came from the same lips that now
praise.

Purity fills me to the brim.
I'm overflowing with salvation
draining from His wrists.

It is remedial, the way your presence flows. Abundance. Fullness of waves in a storm.

This isn't so bad. Not when the pressure is splashing on my skin like this. Vicious. It's so vicious. I'm almost afraid.

But, that's not necessary, is it?

I was raised in fear. We live in an age with our guns locked and loaded, our anxiety inhabiting our most darkest crevices.

And I have too many darkest crevices to count.

But you don't mind, do you? You're not even disgusted, are you?

You knew this about me before I even did. I'm an infant just born. I know how to breathe because it is my instinct. You know I breathe to live. This is why you're so trustworthy. When I'm blind, at least I can say, you have the map of the entire solar system memorized, and you still took the time to learn of my crevices. My oozings. The veins I'm connected too that I'll always be ashamed of.

But it's not necessary, is it?

What does shame do but make me fear the oceans?

I don't want to fear your presence, your ferociousness that roars louder than my hesitations.

Overflowing. Overwhelming. All over me. Even as I write this in an English classroom as I pick a splinter out of my finger. I hear you shouting to me. Like a flirting lover. A smitten heart that can't stop smiling. A slaughtered lamb with arms stretched wide. Like a love note from across the desk, with my name on the envelope.

I am romanced. I am free. I am so in love. Yes, you can take me out, of this world, into the heavens, to the city streets, passed my comfort zones, and anywhere else you'd like.

- C

HANGMAN'S NOOSE

My repentance was Jesus kneeling at my feet
with a wet sponge.

Like when He gave Judas a piece of bread
in front of the disciples.

Like accepting a blessing even though I knew
I'd betray again.

Like walking out of Eden as God played
the goodbye trumpet to Adam and Eve.

He said my sin is in the grave.
I guess I define myself by sin.

Because the guilt is eating me alive.

I take a bite of bread and kiss His wet cheeks,

but I don't want to hang.
I don't want to hang.
I don't want to hang.

i can still hear your cries   from when you died.
       you drowned

in the despair of all sin.   it's mingled in the air.

your whisper   "it is finished"

      is louder than my shouted

apologies.

         i breathe in your sacrifice.

i breathe in your death.

     in your hands, i commit to you

all that i am.   for you are able.

      your hands are more able

   than mine

to set a statue of virtue

      in place again.

your grave made it's mark

       and the world still trembles

   from your last words.

we burn from the remnants

     of our own hells.

your loving,   dying,   fading lungs

       will save us from

ourselves.

THE THINGS YOU WRITE WHEN YOU FACE YOUR DEMONS

showers are sick of being a metaphor. let them live as their own creature. they have nothing to do with how he hurt you. how she hurt you. how the world hates you. what a selfish declaration, to say they are our source of cleansing. like our spirits can't go on without their downpour. to force them to touch our dirt because we're too scared to do it ourselves. as though they really want to hug us in our nakedness to rub off our wretchedness. like it's an honor to behold our vulnerability. they're plagued with all the secrets they've walked in on, but we never meant to be such a mess. and we'd rather sink our heads under and forget what we're ashamed of. we can't look at what we're not proud of. no, this isn't about a shower. but i wrote it in the shower. it could be about a shower. on the surface, it really is about a shower. all i know is, when i told God i needed a friend, i thought to myself: it is here, stripped and swallowing the purity that promises to wipe my skin of all the awful things i've done, that i found one. and that's such a pathetic way to think. and a terrible way to live. to feed off something else so the loneliness doesn't eat me whole.

Remade

spoil me in Your compassion
never ending grace
tendrils of love like
delicate locks of hair
stirring me into a tranquil state

pierce through the silence
when i sit in the valleys
listening to the growling in the bushes
beasts of prey
i shake in fear with the leaves

don't leave me lost in the desert
my throat filled with sand
hungry for all the words i wish i could eat
regret sinks in like a plague but
without waver, You instantly cure me

look at what i've done; the mess i made
knee deep in sorrow and shame
but You see my surrender as
the ultimate treasure
and You cloak me in Your favor
like i never failed at all

THE TASTE OF SNOW

It was cold that day
in the mouth of every Roman
under the tongue of Peter
in the hands of Judas.

I can only imagine
the eerie silence in the cheers
as they whipped a Man
who didn't fight back.

I wonder of His eyes
as He knew what was coming,
if they were empty
angry
or both.

(More importantly
were the sinners able to look in them
without regretting what they were
doing.)

They stood beneath the blizzard
and savored the flavor
the freezing bitter
and shouted for murder.

They stuck their tongues out greedily
as the flakes fell down
to fuel their obscenity
as Mary choked on
her grief.

When He trembled
and walked through the crowd
every drop of blood
for His enemy's redemption,
when He fell under our sin
the wooden splinters sinking in,
when He left the earth
in shakes -

We all tasted snow.
Every past, present, and future soul.
A bitter clump in our throat
as He whispered
"It is finished"
when it was our fault
in the first place.

Regret can be a chilly sting.
Chunky cold rain drops
stuck between our teeth.

But I recall now
just how His eyes looked
and they're not angry.
They're looking at me,
melting the guilt
wiping away the shame
and reminding me
this was all done
so I could be saved.

Motif

she is clothed in pieces of armor.
scraps and rubble. whatever she could find
in the debris of her exploding sorrow.

she is soft and gentle.
her heart is frail to warriors
and closed to her lovers.

she hoards crosses in her back pocket.
to kiss and taste. to devour them
whenever she is empty.

she has skin like a lamp shade.
too hesitant to reveal her flame.
it might blow out in her vulnerability.

she shows grace in her fingertips.
love in her silence. her tongue
speaks only life to her sadness.

she is resilient. she is beautiful.
her vessel may be cracked
but her soul is healing.

The Morning After Relapse

He took my creaking bones
grabbed them with tender palms
and poured oil on my dying carcass
kissing every joint to revive me
from my weariness.

His touch is forgiving but
His love is passionate
and with each drop I
am paralyzed in fascination.

BODY BUILDER

I unlearn chafed palms and sweaty knees.
I teach my heart a new way to pulse, and
it reverberates with less anxious force and
more like silky waves. It tastes like a sleek
wedding dress a bride wears for the first time.
She sighs. And her heart forces one
anxious pound, savoring the memory the only
way she knows how.

I unlearn clenching and tightening and only
praying when I'm desperate. God keeps placing
me where my hands won't hush up,
and I swear to you,
they whisper in their dancing.
I am reminded of my smallness,
my stickily painted skin like battered roses
drenched in red. I feel the most beautiful this way,
but does a lamb's blood really stain
or just wash me into what I have always been?
Oh God. Oh God.

I unlearn muscle tears and twisted joints.
I earnestly strengthen and realign.

Thank God for those shaking hands. For those
anxious pounds. For those hard jaws and cuts on my
thumbs that won't stop oozing my deliverance.
Oh God. Oh God. Oh God.

He's made me a body builder. A muscle of
redeeming scripture. I've never lifted so much,
never risen this high, never stood like this
with so much on my shoulders.
I've never felt as confident as I do now,
holding pebbles in one hand,
a sling in the other,
and my chest pounding anxiously,
the only way it knows how.
Boom. Boom. Boom.
Release the doves and all their
downcast souls. For I am alive more now than I
have ever been.
I don't need them to comfort me anymore.
Oh God. Oh God.

They really mean it when they say
You mold us into something new.

Oh God. Oh God. Oh God.

Washed

i wasn't ridden with
anxiety, it was written
in my bones, it was
a boiling fire taking
over my soul
i couldn't breathe
i couldn't breathe
i had no one to save me
but now i have a
reason to sing
for You are here
better than angels wings
to whisk me from
such pain. You did more
than take me away,
You took my nights
and made them days
and i can sit in the same
places where i begged
for death and say
yes, i have a God
and He saves me
with a joy everlasting.

THE ULTIMATE UNREQUITED LOVE

I would have told Hosea to leave her.

No one should have to hold on, I'd say, to a heart that doesn't want them back.

No one deserves a straying soul, a fleeting kiss, someone who devotes themselves more to the dirt than ever to him.

There are better woman with less stains on their clothes, I'd convince him, they will love you like you deserve.

You shouldn't have to crucify your sainthood for the sake of her.

I would have told Hosea to leave her. But I'm glad he wouldn't have listened.

Because how many times have I deserved to be forsaken? How long have I fought off my destiny of being loved unconditionally?

Since my first breath, born with clenched fists, I've lived half in the shadows, half in my idols, half in the worth I find by giving myself away to temporary places.

How many times have I been an imperfect bride?

I'm a goner, I'm Gomer, and I would have left me a long time ago. But instead of moving on, God never did, for His grace covers me more than my mistakes ever could.

I Wrote This When I Forgot Who God Was

when i asked him "who are you?", he didn't make me feel wrath or trembling fear. he didn't reveal my shame or all the reasons i should hide away. instead, he opened the windows of heaven in an instant, like he's been waiting all my life for this moment, and unearthed his supernatural wonder. i was cloaked with a grace that beat the doves, the first breaths, the final ones, and anything else that reaches the highest scale of soft. i was filled with desire in places i didn't know were empty and a burning tremor of this splendor taking over me, such an unworthy vessel.

i said, "i want to know you. not the idea of you, not what others tell me, not what i hope you are. who are you?" and how a writer knows his pen and an artist knows his paint, he showed me with ease, like it was second nature, like he's done this a million times, like this is what he's here for, by implanting love within me for something greater. he showed me a hopeless world and beautiful souls. forgiveness for their greed and lusts wrapped around them like a coat. all the lands, all the tribes, every culture and tongue, both knowing and unknowing of a man that was sacrificed for them, were so otherworldly adored, so cherished, so absolutely lost, so close to being washed clean if they'd let go of their stone hearts.

it was a graveyard down there and i mourned because i was one of them. i surrendered to life and laid myself flat on a cross to make up for all that was wrong. but it was already finished, i was bought and i was won. there's no need for anguish and death anymore.

i asked him, "who are you?" and he threw me a wedding, a party for my newly found revelation at knowing there is more for me than shoving sin under rugs and pretending i'm alright.

"this is it, this is Me" he said as i watched darkness collide with light in an overwhelming, shaking, painful, morphing sort of way, through the eyes of a mighty God.

GRAPEFRUIT

Morning burns on the window's reflection.
An image of all hell breaking loose
through the ecstasy of an orange
sunrise.

I scream at my sin and my ugly
of how tired I am.
My breath tastes like sweet nectar redemption.

On a bloody cross, I bet Christ craved
grapefruit when He hung.

Like, "wait, does anyone else smell grapefruit?"

Like the more He sucked and swallowed,
the less burden I had to live with.

Like with every second closer to His death,
more lost souls asked for sugar
as the earth shook and thunder roared.

He desperately hated the sour,
but it is my salvation I'm hungry for.
So He gladly sinks His teeth in

again, and again, and again.

Untitled IV

i compress you into my inner workings. in the wounds where oxygen won't flow and the corners that have been empty for far too long

39 whippings written across my walls. a sinful crown for you, a royal throne for me

you stand outside my window with jars of tears that you saved, held above your head like a boom box to prove your love for me

bullets, fists, lust, thorns i adore scatter on the floor

let's burn this house down, there's no reason to live here anymore. no need to collect remnants of a fading history now

Human Nature

I wonder, what did He speak of so well
that made the crowds come closer?
I imagine them all sitting criss-cross
applesauce, children being taught,
and their bright eyes lift as they sit in awe
of the wisdom spilling from His mouth.
It must have been so beautiful.
No wonder Mary was so enraptured
that she drowned His feet in oil,
as this great speaker was inside her home
and just a few feet away, she listened.
What did He speak of so fluently that
brought in those wandering like herding sheep?
Or are we truly all such romantics
that the entire land knew of this Man
because He couldn't stop talking about love?
No wonder we can't let Him go,
after centuries of His tales passing down.
We're all hungry for something,
empty or longing, and in the end,
it's the desire to be otherworldly adored.
It's wanting to know we are loved.

Untitled V

it's all so romantic: from the look on his face when you go to
him broken, to his gentle yet overwhelming presence.

redemption drills in your heels. a kiss on your sweaty forehead.
remnants of his sacrifice still filter in the air.

his name drenched in vain on your lips. he still desires his
bride, even though she has cold feet.

a moment of silence. a bitter pill swallowed. wafting
forgiveness. release.

I like to think that God melts
when children write Him letters
and maybe He's not as raging
as I like to believe He is.
Maybe He is as real
as my desire to be held
but I push and I push
knowing He has better things to do
than sit with me in my loneliness.

But maybe God is as contradictory
as the peacefulness of rushing waves.
As complex as a man who filled
His lungs with bloody, ravaging sin
and all for us, all for love,
a perfect sacrifice for imperfect souls
so lost they don't even care
that He rose to save them from death.

Maybe God can save the world
the hero of New York
the savior for the sinners.
Maybe He can judge us all.

But also be a ruler of the universe
that feels as much as us
and just as He is wrath and anger
He is also love and comfort
and just as I am hurting
so is He grieving.

Maybe He sighs in awe
at the wonder of a baby first born
or watches us glow in admiration
as a sunset burns on our faces.
Maybe He likes to laugh
until His stomach hurts.
Maybe He cries just as we
when someone we love rejects us.

I like to think that God melts
when children write Him letters
just as He rejoices
when someone new enters heaven.
Maybe He is more than
a deity that hates impurity
that damns the sinners
and cursing mouths
and anything else that doesn't
fit in our boxes well enough.

Maybe He loves us all.
Maybe He adores our souls.
Even when we are doubtful
and fleeting, maybe He enjoys
our existing.

Finally

i see it - an appearance from beyond the stars. a coming from a king long awaited for. a combustion of hearts, not from pain, not from regret, but from an outpouring of grace. i see patched up skin, as Christ enters earth, we become more and more whole again. yes, this is it, where we were meant to be all along. this is what will finally fill our holes. the ground shakes, the trumpet sounds, we all know the drill, and no matter where you are, you will rise and rise and rise, plucked up from the dirt like a gardener pulling out weeds and roots. you'll see Him, face to face. we will see Him, in His glory, wrath, in His rightful place as we all praise the only worthy name. there is no fear for those in such a peaceful trance.

i see His eyes and i see home. i finally feel the light of the unseen world. because just passed His overwhelming return is the future we were created for. i see now. we begin to fade, we are not afraid, we leave for our destiny. the house we live in, the life we made, it begins to unravel and passes away.

we don't have time to say goodbye.

we finally see. there is more than our hurt, our sin, our scrambling for purpose, just below the cliffs of uncertainty and behind the evil seeping out of our skin like sweat, cooling us off from the goodness of Him. it's too much to handle, Love taking us back in one full swoop. and just think, He loves us that much. He won the war between heaven and hell and He dug up our graves, stole the keys to our fate, and is finally ready to take us home. is He as excited as us? we go to Him with a child-like glee, finally in our father's arms, and i see now, i see. He's running towards us as well. "finally home", He thinks. and we celebrate for infinity what He did so we could finally, finally, finally live in His everlasting love.

INTERCEDING FOR MY OWN SOUL

she cocoons in the small of God's back
and He says, enough is enough.
she yelps to the air and the air screams back,
filling her lungs with steel. she swallows.
metal is stronger than flesh and she doesn't want
to be soft again. she doesn't want others to
lose themselves after sinking into her tenderness.
anymore. never again.

that's it, that's what happens:
they let go and jump in.
her walls suffocate them
pink and plush and tall.
and soft.
and they regret ever coming in.

replace her pebbles for muscles
so she can feel something grand again.
to touch the face of heaven in an instant.

Praying From Beyond The Gate

i'm sorry i left you out. i'm sorry that i turned away
and blamed you for leaving. i'm sorry i'm so hopeless
when the horizon is silvering through. when it's so
close to your name. your praise. and i can't get myself
to open my mouth just to say it. to take the step. i'm
sorry that i don't want you even when i do. that when
i do want you i also don't. that my feet are splinter-
ing down the middle of the fence and i end up hating
you for the blood spill. for the mess. for my clean sk-
in torn. i'm sorry the mask is so tight. so much that i
fool myself. i don't even talk like this. i don't sound like
this. i don't recognize my voice. hate stole it from me.
i'm sorry i let the anger make me bitter. i'm sorry i cha-
nged and shouted at you for how it felt. for not feeling
human anymore. i'm sorry for pulling when you reach,
for shutting myself out and wondering why i am
alone. i'm sorry my rebirth into goodness is such a
wrestling match. inconvenient reluctance. it's supposed to
be beautiful but my clutter doesn't work well with surrender.
i'm sorry i'm not worthy of the heart you created. that i'm
wasted, hungry flesh standing outside your front porch.
twisting the door knob. begging for food. cursing you for
closing the door when i was the one who ate the key
and demanded you to stay out of the way.

I am your mustard seed
held tightly between
your index and thumb.
Plant life within me.
I will weep your sowing.
I will accept your breaking.
For I am closer to the sun
each time you mend my pieces.

I am your sparrow
and I do not worry
nestled in the highest wood.
I hunger with rage and know
of the food lying below
the trees.
But I wait.
I am patient.
For you have what is best for me.

I am your evening song.
Even when I am awestruck
at the pain taking over
my bones,
my throat strains the
longest notes
of melody over your glory.

I am yours.
I am yours.
I am yours.

I am afraid
but I do not worry.
I will keep singing
and growing.
For I know the plans you have
are better than my own.

The Daughter's Psalm

i wake to write every morning
with you whispering hymns in my ear
like promises slipping out of angels fingers
as they play harps from my window sill.
and i lay to rest my burdens. they fall free
off the cliffs that i used to fear.
you keep speaking and i keep writing
and we have our own little dance
that others would covet.
the world stops existing for those
beautiful seconds.
and i, a simple mind and trying heart,
learn what it feels like for a mighty power
to touch loneliness. not with strong hands
or demands, but simply with breathing words.

OUR HUMAN INSTINCT TO SURVIVE

my surrender really was a

shaking building

not anything close to a

graceful pitch in an

elevator shaft   (with a three part

plan on why i should live)

or a prettily sculpted

kneel   or a kiss to heaven

after winking at the angels

and thanking God for new mercies

walking away unscathed.

the release was

a live or die, make your choice

a fork in the road but

the middle was so warm.

it was love splitting down my

center, body clawing

at the cement, spirit pulling

but for a dead girl   she was strong.

it was gum stuck on a shoe

and the shoe kind of liked it.

it was admitting that i am so

incredibly human, such a

mess of a being

half of my destiny.

it was undressing

and saying

good luck finding the part

of me that's saved, hidden in

all the cobwebs

but if you do, god, if

you figure out how to get there,

make a home out of my

abandonment

find a bed in my

rebellion,   make my heart

a soft cushion.   i've gotten

so hard,

i could use some

tender company

as i cope with

my weaknesses.

God is "deep" and not as in the metaphorical lines of this poem or in the pain of anxiety beneath my prayers. but "deep" as in overwhelming and overtaking and a tremor so "deep" it leaves me speechless. "deep" like i'm suffocating in the presence of wonder but i wouldn't mind never breathing again. "deep" like He's "deeper" than the pit i dug for myself, "deeper" than the hate in my heart, "deeper" than my body can possess all at once. i need to die before i can inhabit His "deep" entirely. He's so "deep", like the inkiness of a midnight sky, "deep" like the shiver thump in my stomach when my lover walks in, "deep" like a vastness of an ocean that makes me feel so small. He is so bright and big and powerful and almighty. i'm so in love that i'm possessed by shiver thumps whenever i go to Him. it amazes me that He can make something beautiful with my mere, shallow existence. God of the deepest of deeps chose me.

- C

LET ME TELL YOU ABOUT THESE WINGS

he planted a seed in my spine
as a fragile, weary thing.

they say he makes life in graves
but i never believed it.

i was dry rotting in the base
of my coffins. i was asphalt

under the old man's shoes.

but he promised to tear up
every realm and i'm pretty sure

he broke all the rules
the way lovers do

to rip me from hell's core.

and i swear the bird's eye view
as i swooned over my old city lights

was worth the terror before

finally waking up.

i kiss the sky's air.

it's so much fresher up here,

and i pity   the ones on the ground.

He gives you a craving so He can bless you with a taste; a dry throat so He can be your relieving river.

Oh, you lost soul, He'll bring you home, He'll bring you home, so you can watch His wonders.

This is God, in all His ways, in everything He does, ravishing, gracious, loving, loving, loving.

A Sigh of Relief

awestruck wonder fills the room.
evening whistles with the shaded
jaded, ever so wasted hymnal song,
as we hope the moon that holds our
twilight secrets doesn't awaken
long enough to forget all we've
done wrong. but the clouds blacken
like an angry sand storm brewing
turning, preparing to drown us all.

yet night, we fear no more.
so amazed by heavens divinity to
even care of our deserved damnation.
grace bestowed, so in awe,
so in love with the keeper of our
lost souls.

SO, YES. IT FINALLY COMES TO THIS.

THE PRODIGAL WALKS UP THE PORCH STAIRS AND
STOPS AT THE DOOR. SHE STARES AT THE WELCOMING
MAT AND REHEARSES HOW TO SAY THINGS LIKE "HOW
LONG HAS IT BEEN?" AND "YES, I'VE BEEN DOING WELL"
WITHOUT SOUNDING LIKE SHE'S CHOKING.

WE HIDE BEHIND SOFAS AND CHAIRS AND TABLES IN
EXCITEMENT TO SHOUT SURPRISE, AS WE RECALL OUR
OWN EXPERIENCES OF WALKING THROUGH THAT
DOOR WAY AND STANDING ON THAT WELCOMING MAT
AND THE DROWNING BEFORE OUR FIRST BREATH.

AND AS WE SCREAM UNTIL OUR THROATS CAVE IN, WE
THANK GOD THIS EXISTS. BECAUSE WITHOUT IT,
THERE WOULD BE NO SUCH THING AS BLEEDING,
PLUMP, FLESHY HEARTS THAT LIVE SOLELY TO POUR
ONTO THE EMPTY ONES.

At Last

i was so naked in the sanctuary / my name was being called /
like death to a tombstone / like destiny to fear / like two
puzzles meant to be but only one side / was reaching

and God likes being a riddle / mystery revealed in glory / the
drum roll before the kiss / so He can show off to the ants of the
earth / when we lie on the beach / so blind we don't realize /
the sun is Him performing

we are blind, aren't we / even with our shades on / even when
we ask / and ask / sometimes we aren't ready for such crashing
ethereality

but when a heart asks without ceasing / when a dam rips open
/ begging for heaven / oh, i don't think anything gives God
more delight / more excitement / more unadulterated joy /
than a lover coming home from war

Liberation Pt. 2

here's my dislocations, my broken ribs, snapped fingers, the hairs you promised you knew by number falling off my shoulders to lifeless piles.

don't mind me, i'm coughing up last nights sin, reviving it's air so it can run from here, far from where you stand.

here's my heart, sign the papers and the deal is done. not a piece is missing, not a scratch is hidden. everything is in place just as you found it. i trust you'll hold me like blossom, fairy, feather, that of a gentle teacher.

surrender (you plead, heaven's warrior intercedes, the bible stuffed in my bedside table reads).

here's my heart, it fit up my throat from all the stretching it's done. i've choked up a lot of thick mass in my time.

X on my chest, marks the spot for your hands, another name for your book, another child for the crucified lamb.

you warned me of the cost for wanting stronger bones. i still spit out the world, flesh, skin.

autopsy report says, "another body to bury, another soul dead".

and you smile and i smile, our teeth glimmering with the secret of eternity.

The Morning After Relapse

ABOUT THE AUTHOR

Christina Hopp lives in Baltimore, Maryland. She studies Theatre and Creative Writing at Towson University. *The Morning After Relapse* is her first published work.

Contact: christinahopp@yahoo.com

Made in the USA
San Bernardino, CA
18 June 2016